ARE YOU A REFUGEE OR A CITIZEN OF THE KINGDOM?

M. C. BROWN

M. C. BROWN

Copyright © 2025, M. C. BROWN

All rights reserved. No part of this publication may be reproduced, stored in a retrieval system, or transmitted in any form or by any means – electronic, mechanical, photocopy, recording, or any other except for brief quotations in printed reviews without permission of the publisher.

ISBN: 978 – 1 –0684558 – 9 – 6

Published by:

MANIFEST R819 PUBLICATIONS

UK: +44(0)7438475709

USA: +1(347)749-8363

Email: admin@manifestr819.com

www.manifestr819.com

TABLE OF CONTENTS

DEDICATION 5
BOOK OVERVIEW: 7
Introduction 13
   THE QUESTION BEFORE US 13
Chapter 1 17
   UNDERSTANDING THE KINGDOM OF GOD 17
Chapter 2 27
   REFUGEE: A BIBLICAL PORTRAIT 27
Chapter 3 39
   THE MINDSET OF A REFUGEE CHRISTIAN 39
Chapter 4 51
   CITIZEN: EMBRACING YOUR KINGDOM IDENTITY
   51
Chapter 5 65
   SIGNS OF CITIZENSHIP IN THE KINGDOM 65
Chapter 6 77
   FROM ESTRANGED TO ENGRAFTED 77
Chapter 7 89
   REFUGEES BY RELIGION, NOT BY FAITH 89
Chapter 8 95
   WALKING IN KINGDOM AUTHORITY 95
Chapter 9 109
   KINGDOM CULTURE AND CITIZENSHIP CONDUCT
   109

Chapter 10 117
   RETURNING HOME: THE PRODIGAL AND THE
   KINGDOM..117

Chapter 11 123
   THE GLOBAL CHURCH: A COMMUNITY OF
   CITIZENS..123

Chapter 12 131
   THE COST AND REWARD OF KINGDOM
   CITIZENSHIP 131

Chapter 13 139
   BECOMING A CITIZEN TODAY..139

Chapter 14 147
   AN INVITATION TO CITIZENSHIP 147

Conclusion 153
   THE JOURNEY HOME 153

ABOUT THE BOOK...159

DEDICATION

TO ALL THOSE...

Journeying in faith, longing for a place to belong not just in church, but in the Kingdom of God.

MAY YOU FIND YOUR IDENTITY, YOUR CITIZENSHIP, AND YOUR HOME IN CHRIST.

M. C. BROWN

BOOK OVERVIEW:

This book explores the spiritual identity of believers through the metaphor of citizenship and exile. It contrasts the experience of living as a spiritual refugee—disconnected, insecure, uncertain—with that of living as a citizen of God's Kingdom—rooted, empowered, and transformed by Christ.

It challenges readers to examine where they truly belong, who governs their heart, and how their status in God's Kingdom should shape their daily lives.

CHAPTER OUTLINE:

Introduction: The Question of Identity

- What does it mean to be a refugee or a citizen spiritually?

- Why this question matters in a world of dislocation and uncertainty.

- An invitation to self-reflection.

Chapter 1: Understanding the Kingdom of God

- What is the Kingdom of God? (Biblical and theological exploration)

- Jesus' teaching on the Kingdom (e.g., Matthew 6:33, Luke 17:21)

- The already-but-not-yet tension of the Kingdom

Chapter 2: Spiritual Refugees

- Defining spiritual refugees: believers who are unsettled, distant, or disconnected

- Causes: trauma, sin, disappointment with church, spiritual warfare

- Biblical examples: Israelites in exile, the prodigal son

Chapter 3: Citizenship in Heaven

- Philippians 3:20 – "Our citizenship is in heaven…"

- Rights and privileges of Kingdom citizens

- Adoption into God's family (Romans 8:15–17)

Chapter 4: The Journey from Refugee to Citizen

- The process of restoration and return

- Repentance, renewal, and re-establishing relationship with Christ

- The role of the Church as a welcoming home, not a border checkpoint

Chapter 5: Living as a Kingdom Citizen

- Daily habits and mindset of a citizen of God's Kingdom

- Stewardship, humility, and service

- Living by Kingdom values in a secular world

Chapter 6: Borders, Exiles, and the Modern Church

- How churches can unintentionally create "refugees" through judgment, politics, or exclusivity

- Reimagining the Church as an embassy of the Kingdom

Chapter 7: Dual Citizenship and Divided Loyalties

- Navigating earthly responsibilities with Kingdom allegiance

- Jesus' teaching on serving two masters (Matthew 6:24)

- Discerning where your ultimate loyalty lies

Chapter 8: The Return of the King

- The hope and promise of Christ's return

- Living in anticipation as loyal citizens

- The final homecoming: Revelation 21

Chapter 9 – Kingdom Culture and Citizenship Conduct
- *Displaying Heaven's values*
- *Conduct, and*
- *Influence in a broken world*

Chapter 10 – Returning Home: The Prodigal and the Kingdom
- *The heart of the Father*

Chapter 11 – The Global Church: A Community of Citizens

Chapter 12 - The Cost and Reward of Kingdom Citizenship

Chapter 13: Becoming a Citizen Today

Chapter 14 – An Invitation to Citizenship Conclusion: Are You a Refugee or a Citizen?

- An invitation to surrender, step into citizenship, and live in full identity
- Reflection questions for personal or group study

M. C. BROWN

Introduction

THE QUESTION BEFORE US

In times marked by displacement, division, and disillusionment, identity has become one of the most urgent and contested issues of our time. Political refugees, cross borders seeking safety. Cultural refugees search for belonging. Even within the Church, there are those who feel spiritually homeless people who once walked closely with God, but now find themselves wandering, uncertain of where they truly belong.

In every generation, the Church is faced with the challenge of spiritual identity. Today, many believers fill pews and serve in ministries, yet live as though they are spiritual exiles—wandering, unsure of their place, and disconnected from the full privileges of Kingdom life.

This book was born out of a simple thought, yet raises a vital, piercing and searching question: Are you a refugee, or are you a citizen of the Kingdom of God?

It is a question not of nationality, but of spiritual identity. Not of geography, but of belonging. Not of politics, but of allegiance. And it is a question that invites every believer to examine the posture of their heart and the direction of their life

Refugees often live in uncertainty. They seek shelter but lack legal status, rights, and the full experience of belonging. Sadly, many Christians live this way in the spiritual realm. They attend church but don't feel connected. They know of God but haven't discovered what it means to truly belong to Him.

By contrast, citizens of the Kingdom know where they belong. They understand their rights, responsibilities, and identity in Christ.

They don't just visit the Kingdom—they live in it.

Jesus didn't come to start a religion; He came to establish a Kingdom—a spiritual realm where God's will, is done on earth as it is in heaven. Through salvation, Jesus offers us not only forgiveness, but full **citizenship** in this Kingdom.

This book is not about judgment. It is an invitation. An invitation to examine your spiritual posture, and if necessary, to shift from wandering to belonging, from estrangement to identity, from survival to purpose.

So, I ask you again: **Are you a refugee, or are you a citizen in the Kingdom of God?**

If you have ever felt like a spiritual refugee—unsettled, uprooted, uncertain—you are not alone. And you are not without hope.

Jesus didn't come just to forgive our sins—He came to give us a new home, a new name, and a new future. Through His death and resurrection, He made a way for us to move from exile to citizenship, from wandering to belonging.

The journey starts here.

Are you a refugee, or a citizen of the Kingdom of God?

Let's find out—together.

Chapter 1

UNDERSTANDING THE KINGDOM OF GOD

"From that time on Jesus began to preach, 'Repent, for the kingdom of heaven has come near.'" —Matthew 4:17 (NIV)

When Jesus began His public ministry, He did not start with miracles, music, or meetings. He began with a message: **the Kingdom of God has come near.** This phrase was central to His teaching, His miracles, His parables, and His mission. Yet many Christians today have only a vague idea of what the Kingdom truly is.

WHAT IS THE KINGDOM OF GOD?

At its most basic level, the Kingdom of God is the reign and rule of God. It is not confined to geography or politics. It transcends borders and systems. The Kingdom is wherever God's authority is recognised, His will is done, and His presence is welcomed.

Jesus taught His disciples to pray, *"Your Kingdom come, your will be done, on earth as it is in heaven" (Matthew 6:10)*. This was not just a prayer for the future—it was a declaration that God's reign could begin here and now, in real time, in real hearts.

The Kingdom is both present and future. It is already, and it is not yet. This tension can be difficult to grasp, but it's central to Christian life:

- Already: Jesus brought the Kingdom when He came to earth. His miracles, teachings, and resurrection all revealed the power of the Kingdom breaking into our world.

- Not yet: The Kingdom will be fully revealed when Christ returns. Sin, death, and suffering will be no more. Until then, we live as ambassadors in a world that does not fully recognise its true King.

NOT OF THIS WORLD

Jesus once said to Pilate, "My Kingdom is not of this world" (John 18:36). His Kingdom doesn't operate by the logic of power, pride, or domination. It is a Kingdom of humility, love, justice, mercy, and truth.

It is a Kingdom where:
- The last are first.
- The meek inherit the earth.
- The poor in spirit receive everything.
- The peacemakers are called children of God.

This upside-down Kingdom challenges every other allegiance. It exposes the poverty of earthly kingdoms, whether political, cultural, or personal. And it invites us into something far greater: a Kingdom that can never be shaken (Hebrews 12:28).

The Kingdom of God is not merely a distant, future paradise in heaven. It is the present and active **rule and reign of God** wherever His will is being done. It is not confined to geography or governed by human politics. It is spiritual in nature, yet visible in its effects. It exists **wherever Jesus is Lord.**

The Kingdom is:
- **Spiritual** – It lives in the hearts of believers (Luke 17:21).
- **Dynamic** – It grows like a seed, transforming lives and cultures (Mark 4:30–32).
- **Comprehensive** – It affects personal, relational, and societal dimensions.
- **Eternal** – It cannot be shaken or overthrown (Hebrews 12:28).

Jesus demonstrated the Kingdom by:
- Healing the sick (Matthew 9:35)
- Forgiving sins (Luke 5:24)
- Casting out demons (Matthew 12:28)
- Teaching truth with authority (Mark 1:22)

Every miracle was a signpost pointing to the Kingdom's arrival and power.

THE COST OF THE KINGDOM

Jesus told a parable of a man who found treasure hidden in a field. In his joy, he sold everything he had to buy that field (Matthew 13:44). That's what the Kingdom is like: it's worth everything. But to receive it, something must be surrendered.

To become citizens of the Kingdom of God, we must lay down our own crowns. We must renounce our allegiance to self-rule and come under the gracious lordship of Christ. This is not about oppression—it is about liberation. For where Christ reigns, there is freedom.

Yet many reject the Kingdom because they prefer the illusion of control. Others admire the idea of the Kingdom but hesitate to enter fully. Jesus is clear: we cannot serve two masters. We must choose whom we will follow, whom we will trust, and where we will find home.

KINGDOM DNA

Every kingdom has its culture—its laws, language, and values. The Kingdom of God is no different. It has its own "DNA"—a way of life shaped not by rules but by relationship with the King.

The Kingdom is marked by:
- Righteousness – living in right relationship with God and others
- Peace – deep, inner wholeness and outward reconciliation
- Joy – the fruit of knowing we are loved and secure in Christ (*see* Romans 14:17)

This Kingdom is not a weekend religion. It is a whole-life reality. It shapes how we treat others, spend our time, forgive enemies, handle money, and make decisions. It changes us from the inside out.

THE KINGDOM IS A PERSON
Ultimately, the Kingdom of God is not an abstract idea—it is found in a Person. Wherever Jesus is acknowledged as Lord, the Kingdom is present. He is the King who brings the Kingdom.

> ➤ To receive the Kingdom, we must receive Him.

> To follow the Kingdom way, we must follow Him.
> To dwell in the Kingdom, we must dwell in Him.

THE KINGDOM AND THE CHURCH

The Church is not the Kingdom, but it is the **vehicle** through which the Kingdom is expressed on earth. The Church gathers citizens of the Kingdom and equips them to live under the Lordship of Christ and extend His reign in the world.

- The **Kingdom** is the **reign** of God.
- The **Church** is the **representation** of that reign on earth.

To belong to the Church without submitting to the Kingdom is to participate in form without power.

ENTRY INTO THE KINGDOM

Citizenship in this Kingdom is not inherited through family, nationality, or tradition. It is **received** through repentance and faith in Jesus Christ.

"Very truly I tell you, no one can see the kingdom of God unless they are born again." —John 3:3 (NIV)

You cannot enter by works, effort, or religion. Only those who are born again—spiritually reborn through the Holy Spirit—can perceive and participate in the Kingdom.

This new birth is not just a ticket to heaven; it is an entrance into a **new realm of life** governed by a new King.

LIVING UNDER KINGDOM RULE

To be in the Kingdom means to live in willing submission to King Jesus. This affects:

- Your **priorities**: *"Seek first the Kingdom of God..."* (Matthew 6:33)
- Your **values**: Loving enemies, serving the poor, walking humbly
- Your **decisions**: Living in obedience and integrity
- Your **identity**: No longer slaves to sin, but sons and daughters of God

Kingdom life is radically different from worldly life. It is a call to transformation, not just attendance.

KINGDOM CITIZENS ARE KINGDOM AMBASSADORS

As believers, we are more than just members of a church—we are **ambassadors of the Kingdom** (2 Corinthians 5:20). We represent our King wherever we go, carrying the message, the power, and the presence of God into every sphere of life.

The question, then, is not just: *Do you go to church?*
But rather: *Do you live under the reign of Christ? Are you part of His Kingdom?*

This foundational chapter sets the stage for what follows. You cannot understand the difference between a refugee and a citizen unless you first understand **what the Kingdom truly is**.

REFLECTION:

- Do you see the Kingdom of God as something distant or present?

- In what areas of your life is Jesus not yet fully ruling?

- What might it look like for you to live under the reign of Christ more fully?

The Kingdom of God is not a someday reality for a select few. It is a here-and-now invitation for all who are willing to surrender to the King. This Kingdom is your inheritance—if you choose to receive it.

The question remains: Are you living as a subject of this Kingdom, or as a spiritual refugee searching for another home?

Chapter 2

REFUGEE: A BIBLICAL PORTRAIT

"Remember that at that time you were separate from Christ... foreigners to the covenants of the promise, without hope and without God in the world." — Ephesians 2:12 (NIV)

The image of a refugee is one of displacement. It speaks of people who have been **uprooted from their homes**, **disconnected from legal rights**, and **forced into survival mode**. The Bible is filled with stories of people who were, for a time, spiritual or physical refugees—and their experiences teach us vital lessons.

Imagine a person who once had a home—a place of security, identity, and belonging. But something happened. A conflict. A crisis. A loss. Now they are displaced, unsure of where they belong or who they are. This is the plight of a refugee.

Spiritually speaking, many believers live like this. They once walked closely with God. They experienced His peace and purpose. But now, they feel distant, disconnected, and spiritually homeless.

They may attend church, read their Bible, or try to pray—but inside, they feel like wanderers. They are no longer rooted in the Kingdom of God. They feel like exiles in a land that once felt like home.

WHO ARE SPIRITUAL REFUGEES?

A spiritual refugee is not someone outside of God's reach. In fact, many spiritual refugees once knew Him deeply. But now they feel lost—not because God left them, but because something in their journey disrupted their sense of belonging.

These are people who:

- Have been hurt by the church
- Feel burned out by religious performance
- Wrestle with doubt or unanswered prayers
- Carry shame from past sin or failure
- Struggle to experience God's presence

They long to belong again, but they aren't sure how. They know the language of faith but feel disconnected from its power. They believe in the Kingdom but feel like they're watching it from a distance.

Scripture is full of stories of exile—of people who were physically or spiritually displaced, yet deeply loved by God.

1. The Israelites in Exile
After years of disobedience, God's people were taken into Babylonian captivity. They were far from the land God promised, surrounded by pagan culture, and grieving what they had lost.

In exile, they asked:

"How can we sing the Lord's song in a foreign land?" (Psalm 137:4).

Yet even in exile, God did not abandon them. He sent prophets like Jeremiah and Ezekiel to speak hope. He promised restoration. He reminded them: *"I know the plans I have for you... plans to prosper you and not to harm you" (Jeremiah 29:11).*

2. The Prodigal Son

Jesus told a story of a young man who left his father's house in search of freedom. He wasted his inheritance, ended up feeding pigs, and realised he had lost everything. He was a refugee—not only in a foreign country, but in his soul.

But when he returned, the father ran to him, embraced him, and restored him (Luke 15). This is the heart of God toward all spiritual refugees. He doesn't shame them—He welcomes them.

3. Elijah in the Wilderness

After a great spiritual victory, the prophet Elijah fled in fear and ended up in a cave, asking God to take his life (1 Kings 19). He felt isolated, forgotten, and spiritually numb.

But God came to him—not in wind or fire, but in a still, small voice. Elijah wasn't condemned for his weakness. He was renewed by God's presence.

4. The Israelites in the Wilderness

Perhaps the most vivid example of a spiritual refugee condition is found in the Israelites after their exodus from Egypt. Though physically free from slavery, they **lacked the mindset and maturity** to enter the Promised Land.

They were:
- Fearful of giants
- Longing for Egypt
- Grumbling and complaining
- Quick to turn to idols

They had left **Egypt,** but **Egypt had not left them.** They were caught between deliverance and destiny—wandering, unsure, rebellious. They were no longer slaves, but not yet citizens. They were spiritual refugees.

"They are a people whose hearts go astray, and they have not known my ways." (Psalm 95:10, NIV)

Refugee Christians live in this in-between state. They are out of sin, but not yet rooted in sonship. They know about God, but do not walk with Him confidently.

5. Ruth – A Refugee Redeemed

The story of Ruth shows another aspect. She was a literal refugee—a Moabite widow who followed her mother-in-law Naomi back to Bethlehem. She was an outsider, grieving, and vulnerable. But through her **decision to follow Naomi's God**, and her faithfulness, she was **redeemed, restored, and received** into God's people.

"Your people will be my people and your God my God." (Ruth 1:16, NIV)

Ruth went from refugee to covenant participant—not by force, but by **faith and relationship**.

6. Refugee Christianity Today

In our time, many believers resemble spiritual refugees:

- They attend church but don't feel connected.
- They serve, but without joy.
- They struggle to believe they are truly accepted or wanted.
- They live as though God is a distant provider, not a loving Father.

A refugee Christian often feels like they are just *passing through* church, never *planted* in it. They move from one ministry to another, seeking shelter but never settling in sonship.

Signs of a refugee mindset include:
- **Fear of commitment** – avoiding membership, accountability, or vulnerability
- **Spiritual insecurity** – always wondering if they are "good enough".
- **Transient faith** – never fully rooted or growing.
- **Defensiveness or mistrust** – shaped by past wounds or rejections.

Refugees may know the language of the Church but not the **culture of the Kingdom**.

A FALSE SENSE OF SAFETY

Some live under the illusion that religious involvement equals Kingdom citizenship. But religion can mask deep spiritual disconnection. You can be active in the church but absent from the Kingdom.

"These people honour me with their lips, but their hearts are far from me." —Matthew 15:8 (NIV)

God does not want us to live as spiritual refugees. He desires to **bring us home**, to plant us in His house, and to give us identity and inheritance.

CAUSES OF SPIRITUAL DISPLACEMENT

Understanding how people become spiritual refugees is key to helping them return home.

- Wounds from Church or Leaders: Abuse, betrayal, or toxic leadership can drive people away from community and faith.

- Religious Burnout: When faith becomes performance, people grow tired, feeling like they're never enough.

- Sin and Shame: Hidden sin or unresolved guilt can cause believers to withdraw from God out of fear.

- Doubt and Disillusionment: When life doesn't go as expected, faith can feel fragile or even fraudulent.

- Isolation: A lack of meaningful connection with other believers can make faith feel dry and empty.

GOD'S HEART FOR THE REFUGEE

Throughout Scripture, God shows special concern for the refugee, the outsider, the lost.

"The Lord watches over the foreigner and sustains the fatherless and the widow" (Psalm 146:9).

Jesus Himself was a refugee—fleeing with His parents to Egypt as an infant (Matthew 2:13-15).

And spiritually, Jesus came to seek and save the lost (Luke 19:10).

He doesn't ignore the displaced—He draws near to them. He leaves the 99 to find the one. He prepares a place at the table for the one who feels they don't belong.

The journey from spiritual exile to citizenship doesn't begin with striving—it begins with surrender.

God doesn't ask you to clean yourself up before returning. He invites you to come just as you are.

If you've been living like a spiritual refugee:

- Know that God sees you.
- Know that He still loves you.
- Know that He has not revoked your invitation to the Kingdom.

You are not beyond redemption. You are not forgotten. You are not disqualified. The door is open. The Father is waiting. The Kingdom is calling.

REFLECTION:

- Have you ever felt like a spiritual refugee? What led to that feeling?

- Are there wounds or disappointments you haven't yet brought to God?

- What would it look like for you to begin returning to the Father today?

Being a refugee is not your final identity. It is a temporary condition that God longs to redeem. Jesus did not die for you to wander aimlessly — He died to bring you home.

M. C. BROWN

> *In the next chapter, we will look more closely at the **mindset of a refugee Christian** and how it affects our faith, our growth, and our ability to receive from God.*

Chapter 3

THE MINDSET OF A REFUGEE CHRISTIAN

"The Israelites said to them, 'If only we had died by the Lord's hand in Egypt! There we sat around pots of meat and ate all the food we wanted, but you have brought us out into this desert to starve this entire assembly to death.'" —Exodus 16:3 (NIV)

The physical journey out of Egypt was miraculous—but the emotional and mental journey was much slower. God had delivered the Israelites, but **they still thought like slaves**. Their hearts and minds remained in Egypt. This is the dilemma of many believers today. While they have received Christ, their **mindset is still that of a refugee.**

A refugee mindset limits how you see God, yourself, others, and your future. Let's explore the key characteristics of this mindset.

1. Spiritual Insecurity

A refugee Christian often questions whether they truly belong. They may believe they are saved but live as though they are still being evaluated. Instead of walking in assurance, they wrestle with fear of rejection:

- "Does God really love me?"
- "Am I worthy enough?"
- "What if I fail again?"

This insecurity leads to performance-based Christianity, where spiritual activity is used to try and earn God's favour rather than living from a place of accepted grace.

"The Spirit you received does not make you slaves, so that you live in fear again; rather, the Spirit you received brought about your adoption to sonship." — Romans 8:15 (NIV)

2. Fear of Commitment

Refugees are cautious. They've been displaced and wounded. Spiritually, this translates into believers who fear:

- Joining a local church fully
- Submitting to spiritual leadership
- Opening up to others in community
- Entering long-term spiritual relationships

Instead of growing deep roots, they stay on the surface, moving from one place or pastor to another when discomfort arises. But Kingdom life requires covenant—not convenience.

3. Survival Mode Spirituality

Refugee-minded believers are always spiritually "on the run." Their walk with God is not marked by abundance or joy but by struggle and survival.

- Prayer becomes a duty, not a delight.
- Worship becomes emotional escape, not revelation.
- Service becomes burnout, not blessing.

They are constantly doing but rarely resting in their identity as children of God. The goal becomes survival, not transformation.

4. Defensiveness and Distrust

Having experienced hurt or displacement—whether from churches, leaders, or fellow believers—refugee Christians often guard themselves with suspicion. They struggle to:

- Receive correction
- Trust spiritual authority
- Walk in spiritual vulnerability

This makes discipleship difficult and healing delayed. A refugee mindset often builds walls instead of bridges, fearing that openness will lead to more wounds.

5. A Wandering Spirit

Just as the Israelites circled the wilderness for 40 years, refugee-minded Christians often go in circles spiritually:

- Repeating the same battles
- Revisiting the same sins

- Rehearsing the same doubts

They want change, but are not yet ready to trust the process of God's transformation. They long for the Promised Land but struggle to leave the comfort of survival.

MOVING BEYOND THE REFUGEE MINDSET

God is not angry with the refugee-minded believer—He is **calling them to more**. He is patient, loving, and persistent. But He will not allow us to stay in the wilderness when He has prepared a place of **citizenship, sonship, and settlement**.

"You were taught... to be made new in the attitude of your minds; and to put on the new self, created to be like God in true righteousness and holiness." — Ephesians 4:22–24 (NIV)

Transformation begins not with location, but with the **renewing of the mind**. The longer we think like refugees, the longer we will live beneath the fullness of the Kingdom.

In a world of shifting identities and fragile allegiances, the Apostle Paul offers a bold declaration:

"But our citizenship is in heaven. And we eagerly await a Savior from there, the Lord Jesus Christ." (Philippians 3:20, NIV)

This one sentence carries profound implications. It tells us not only where we belong, but to whom we belong. It tells us that as followers of Christ, we are not just survivors or wanderers — we are citizens of an eternal Kingdom, with all the rights, responsibilities, and privileges that citizenship implies.

But what does it really mean to be a citizen of heaven? And how does that identity shape how we live on earth?

1. The Nature of Kingdom Citizenship

Citizenship is about more than where you live — it's about where you belong. It means you have legal standing, protection under the law, and a place in the national story. It's a matter of identity and allegiance.

To be a citizen of heaven means that your primary identity, loyalty, and sense of belonging are found not in this world, but in God's Kingdom. You live here, but you belong there.

As Jesus said to His disciples: *"You do not belong to the world, but I have chosen you out of the world."* *(John 15:19)*

2. Citizenship Is Received; Not Earned Earthly citizenship is often inherited or achieved. But heavenly citizenship is received by grace.

- You do not earn it by good works.
- You are not disqualified by your past.
- It is given freely to all who put their trust in Jesus Christ.

As Paul writes in Ephesians 2:19: *"You are no longer foreigners and strangers, but fellow citizens with God's people and also members of His household."*

You may have once been a spiritual refugee, but through Christ, you are now a full citizen—fully accepted, fully included, fully secure.

3. The Rights of Kingdom Citizens

Citizenship in heaven comes with remarkable privileges—ones that surpass any earthly nation's benefits.

a. A New Identity

You are now a child of God, not defined by your failures or your past. You have been adopted into the family of the King (Romans 8:15–17).

b. Eternal Security

No power in heaven or on earth can take your citizenship away (Romans 8:38–39). Your place in God's Kingdom is secured by Christ's blood.

c. Access to the King

Unlike earthly kings, your Heavenly King is always accessible. You can approach God with confidence (Hebrews 4:16).

d. Inheritance and Purpose

You have a royal inheritance and a mission. You are called to reflect Kingdom values and participate in God's redemptive work (1 Peter 2:9).

4. The Responsibilities of Kingdom Citizens

Heavenly citizenship also comes with responsibilities. Just as earthly citizens are expected to uphold laws and contribute to the good of their nation, Kingdom citizens are called to live differently.

a. Live as Ambassadors

You represent your King wherever you go. Paul writes, *"We are therefore Christ's ambassadors, as though God were making His appeal through us" (2 Corinthians 5:20).* Your words, actions, and attitudes should reflect the heart of the Kingdom.

b. Seek First the Kingdom

Jesus said, *"Seek first the Kingdom of God and His righteousness" (Matthew 6:33).* Your priorities should be shaped by God's values, not worldly pressures.

c. Obey the King's Commands

Obedience is not about legalism—it's about love. Jesus said, *"If you love me, keep my commands" (John 14:15).* Citizenship means surrendering to His authority and trusting His ways.

d. Love Fellow Citizens

In God's Kingdom, citizenship is not individualistic—it's communal. You belong to a people. You are called to love, forgive, serve, and walk with others in grace and truth (Galatians 6:2).

5. Living Between Two Worlds

Though your citizenship is in heaven, your location is still on earth. This creates a kind of holy tension. You are both a resident of earth and a citizen of heaven. You are living in the "already but not yet"—redeemed by Christ but still surrounded by brokenness.

This calls for discernment:

- Will you live by the values of this world or those of the Kingdom?

- Will you pursue status in earthly systems or invest in eternal treasure?

- Will you conform to the culture around you or be transformed by the Spirit?

6. Kingdom Citizenship in a Divided World

In times of political, cultural, and moral division, Kingdom citizenship becomes even more essential. It reminds us that our ultimate allegiance is not to a nation, political party, or ideology, but to Jesus Christ, the King of Kings.

This doesn't mean we ignore the world's needs or abandon civic duties. Rather, we engage them as Kingdom citizens—grounded in truth, guided by grace, and motivated by love.

REFLECTION:

- Do you live with the confidence that you are a citizen of heaven?

- Are there areas in your life where your loyalty is more to the world than to God's Kingdom?

- How would your choices and attitudes change if you fully embraced your Kingdom citizenship?

You are no longer a stranger. No longer a wanderer. Through Christ, you have been given a passport stamped with grace. You are a citizen of the Kingdom of God. Live like it. Love like it. Let the world see the light of your true homeland.

Chapter 4
CITIZEN: EMBRACING YOUR KINGDOM IDENTITY

"But our citizenship is in heaven. And we eagerly await a Saviour from there, the Lord Jesus Christ."
—*Philippians 3:20 (NIV)*

When we come to Christ, we do not just receive forgiveness—we are given **a new identity and a new citizenship**. We become part of something eternal, divine, and unshakable. No longer spiritual refugees, we are now **citizens of the Kingdom of God**.

This truth should radically shape how we think, how we live, and how we relate to God, the Church, and the world.

WHAT DOES IT MEAN TO BE A KINGDOM CITIZEN?

A citizen is more than a resident. A resident may live in a place, but a citizen belongs. A citizen:

- Has rights and privileges under a nation's law
- Owes allegiance to its government or king
- Participates in the life and responsibility of the nation

Spiritually, Kingdom citizens:

- Live under the rule of Christ
- Possess spiritual authority and access
- Represent the King in all they do
- Belong fully in the family of God

We are no longer **outsiders**. We are **sons and daughters**, **ambassadors**, and **heirs** of the Kingdom.

"Consequently, you are no longer foreigners and strangers, but fellow citizens with God's people and

also members of his household." —Ephesians 2:19 (NIV)

THE BENEFITS OF KINGDOM CITIZENSHIP

Being a citizen of the Kingdom comes with blessings that surpass anything this world can offer:

1. **Legal Status in Christ.** You are not trying to earn God's approval—you already have it through Jesus. You are accepted in the Beloved (Ephesians 1:6). No longer on probation, you are fully welcomed.
2. **Access to the King.** You can approach God with freedom and confidence (Hebrews 4:16). You have the Holy Spirit within you as your Helper, Guide, and Seal of ownership.
3. **Spiritual Authority.** You carry the name, authority, and backing of Heaven. You can rebuke darkness, walk in power, and pray with Kingdom impact.
4. **Family Identity.** You belong to a global and eternal family. You are not alone. You

are part of the Body of Christ and God's household.
5. **Inheritance and Purpose.** You have a Kingdom assignment and a future. Your life is not random—you have been called "for such a time as this."

CHARACTERISTICS OF A KINGDOM CITIZEN

How do Kingdom citizens live? What distinguishes them from spiritual refugees? They are:

- **Rooted** – Planted in the Word and in a local church
- **Secure** – Not moved by fear or opinion because they know whose they are
- **Obedient** – Living under the Lordship of Jesus, not led by the flesh
- **Purposeful** – Serving in their calling, blessing others, making disciples
- **Fruitful** – Bearing the fruit of the Spirit (Galatians 5:22–23)

Citizens don't just attend church—they carry the Kingdom **with them and within them**. Their lives reflect Heaven's values.

THE JOURNEY FROM REFUGEE TO CITIZEN

Becoming a citizen of God's Kingdom is a **process of revelation and transformation**. It begins the moment you put your faith in Christ, but must continue as you:

- Renew your mind with God's Word
- Embrace the work of the Holy Spirit
- Submit to God's rule and righteous standards
- Allow the Church to disciple and equip you

This is not merely behavioural change—it is **identity transformation**. You stop striving and start living from the truth that **you are already accepted, adopted, and assigned.**

"The Spirit himself testifies with our spirit that we are God's children. Now if we are children, then we are heirs..." —Romans 8:16–17 (NIV)

GOD WANTS YOU TO SETTLE

Citizens are settled. They have an address. God is calling you to **move from spiritual wandering to spiritual settlement.** No more living like a guest in the house of God—you are a rightful member.

Your place is not just at the altar but **at the table.** Your posture is not just kneeling in desperation but **standing in confidence.** You are not hoping to be chosen—you already have been.

"You did not choose me, but I chose you and appointed you..." —John 15:16 (NIV)

Becoming a citizen of the Kingdom of God is not just a change of status—it is a transformation of the heart. It is a journey. And like any journey, it involves movement, moments of decision, and seasons of growth.

No one stumbles into Kingdom citizenship by accident. We may begin our spiritual lives as wanderers, wounded or confused, but God graciously invites us to come home—to leave behind spiritual exile and step into full belonging.

1. The Awakening: Recognizing Your Displacement

Every journey begins with awareness. Before we can move forward, we must first recognise where we are.

For many spiritual refugees, life becomes marked by:

- Restlessness: – an inner ache for something more.
- Disconnection: – a sense of distance from God, His people, or His presence.
- Weariness: – from striving, pretending, or carrying unresolved pain.

This is the moment of awakening. Like the prodigal son in the pigpen, we come to ourselves and realise: "This is not where I belong."

God often uses pain, failure, or longing to stir this awakening. It is not a sign of rejection—it is a sign of invitation. God is calling you back.

2. The Turning: Repentance and Surrender

Awareness alone is not enough. The next step is repentance—not just sorrow, but a change in direction.

Repentance is not merely about feeling bad—it is about turning around. It is the decision to stop running, stop hiding, stop blaming, and return to the Father.

Jesus said, *"Repent, for the Kingdom of heaven is at hand"* (Matthew 4:17). Repentance opens the door to Kingdom life. It means laying down pride, self-reliance, and sin. It is not easy, but it is necessary.

This is where many get stuck. They feel unworthy, afraid, or unsure how to return. But remember this:

The Kingdom is not for those who get it all right. It's for those who admit they can't—and run to the One who did.

3. The Embrace: Receiving Grace and Identity

When a refugee returns, God does not meet them with a list of rules—He meets them with open arms.

In the parable of the prodigal son, the father ran to meet his son, clothed him, fed him, and celebrated him. That's how God responds to every returning heart.

This stage of the journey is all about receiving grace:
- You are forgiven.
- You are accepted.
- You are loved.
- You are no longer a stranger—you are a citizen, a child, an heir.

Don't rush this part. Let God rewire your thinking. Let Him restore your identity. Let Him heal the wounds that exile left behind.

4. The Formation: Growing in Kingdom Life

Becoming a citizen is not the end—it is the beginning. Now the real journey begins: living into the reality of your new home.

This involves:

- Discipleship – learning to follow Jesus daily, in all areas of life.

- Community – connecting with other believers, walking together in grace and truth.

- Obedience – responding to the King's voice with trust, even when it's hard.

- Transformation – allowing the Spirit to renew your mind, character, and purpose.

Spiritual formation is not about perfection—it's about progress. The Kingdom shapes you gradually, like yeast in dough or seeds in soil (Matthew 13).

The goal is not to look religious—it's to look like Jesus.

5. The Witness: Living as an Ambassador

As your identity is rooted in Kingdom citizenship, your life becomes a witness. You don't just carry a title—you carry a mission.

You are now an ambassador of the Kingdom:

- You speak hope where there is despair.
- You bring peace where there is conflict.
- You live with integrity, love, and courage.
- You invite others into the same journey—from refugee to citizen.

Every act of love, every moment of forgiveness, every stand for truth is a signal of the Kingdom breaking into this world.

6. The Roadblocks and Grace Along the Way

This journey is not without obstacles. Even after returning, you may still feel like a refugee at times. Doubts will come. Old patterns may resurface. Community may disappoint you. The enemy will whisper lies.

But grace remains.

- When you fall, the King does not revoke your citizenship.

- When you doubt, the Spirit intercedes.

- When you feel lost again, the Father still waits with open arms.

Citizenship is not sustained by your strength, but by God's faithfulness.

REFLECTION:
- Have you had a moment of awakening in your life? What prompted it?

- Where are you on the journey—from refugee to citizen?

- What would it mean for you to fully embrace your identity as a citizen of God's Kingdom?

The journey from spiritual exile to Kingdom citizenship is the story of every believer. It is not a path of shame, but of grace. Not of fear, but of freedom.

REFUGEE OR CITIZEN?

If you're still on the road, keep walking. If you've stumbled, get back up. If you've forgotten who you are, let this remind you:

You are no longer a spiritual refugee.
You are a citizen of heaven.
You are home.

*In the next chapter, we'll explore **how to recognise the signs** that someone is truly walking as a citizen of the Kingdom—and how to grow deeper in this powerful identity.*

Chapter 5

SIGNS OF CITIZENSHIP IN THE KINGDOM

"So then, you will know them by their fruits." —
Matthew 7:20 (NIV)

Being a citizen of the Kingdom of God is more than a label—it is a lifestyle. Citizenship in the Kingdom is evidenced not by where we go on Sunday, but by how we live every day. Jesus said we would be known by our *fruit*, not our *words*.

In this chapter, we explore the distinguishing marks of a true Kingdom citizen—those whose lives reveal they are no longer spiritual refugees, but secure, transformed, and walking under the Lordship of Christ.

1. Rootedness in Christ and Community
Kingdom citizens are **planted**, not drifting. They are not blown about by every wind of doctrine, emotion, or disappointment.

"They are like trees planted by streams of water, which yield their fruit in season..." —Psalm 1:3 (NIV)

They:
- Have a consistent walk with God
- Are established in the Word and prayer
- Are committed to a local church
- Serve faithfully and grow in fellowship

Rooted believers don't flee at the first sign of conflict—they stay, grow, and bear fruit.

2. Spiritual Maturity and Growth
A sign of true citizenship is the **visible growth of Christlike character** over time.

"Instead, speaking the truth in love, we will grow to become in every respect the mature body of him who is the head, that is, Christ." —Ephesians 4:15 (NIV)

Citizens are growing in:
- Love
- Patience
- Faithfulness
- Humility
- Forgiveness

They are no longer content with surface-level Christianity. They desire depth, maturity, and the mind of Christ.

3. Walking in Authority and Assurance

Citizens of the Kingdom know who they are and who sent them. They walk in the **spiritual authority** given to them by Christ. *"I have given you authority… to overcome all the power of the enemy; nothing will harm you."* —Luke 10:19 (NIV)

They are not tossed by fear or the opinions of others. They know:
- They are sons and daughters, not slaves
- They have access to the Father

- They carry the presence and backing of Heaven

They speak with boldness, pray with confidence, and live with purpose.

4. Engagement in Kingdom Mission

Citizens don't live for themselves—they live for the King and His purposes.

"We are therefore Christ's ambassadors, as though God were making his appeal through us." —2 Corinthians 5:20 (NIV)

Signs of a Kingdom mission mindset:

- Evangelism and witness are a priority
- Discipleship is embraced, not avoided
- Gifts are used to edify the body and glorify God
- There is a heart for justice, mercy, and truth

Citizens of the Kingdom live on assignment.

5. Fruit of the Spirit

The ultimate evidence of citizenship is **spiritual fruit**, not religious activity. *"But the fruit of the Spirit is love, joy, peace, forbearance, kindness, goodness, faithfulness, gentleness and self-control."* — Galatians 5:22–23 (NIV)

Refugees may perform religious acts out of fear or obligation. Citizens **bear fruit** out of identity and intimacy with God. Their inner transformation leads to outward evidence of the Spirit's work.

6. Submission to Kingdom Values

Kingdom citizens live by Heaven's code of conduct. They embrace the teachings of Jesus, even when countercultural.

They:

- Turn the other cheek
- Love their enemies
- Practice generosity and humility
- Forgive repeatedly
- Seek first the Kingdom of God

Their lives reflect the **values of the King**, not the customs of the world.

7. Perseverance in Trials

True citizens don't abandon their post when life gets hard. They endure, persevere, and grow stronger.

"Blessed is the one who perseveres under trial..."
—James 1:12 (NIV)

A refugee may panic, but a citizen trusts. They don't interpret hardship as rejection. They know God is still working, still faithful, and still present.

A KINGDOM CITIZEN IS NOT PERFECT— BUT IS PROGRESSING.

Kingdom citizenship is not about perfection, but **transformation**. It is not about keeping rules, but growing in **relationship**. God's grace empowers the citizen to reflect the nature of the King.

Not all who claim the Kingdom live as its citizens. Citizenship is more than a status—it is a life transformed by allegiance to Christ. It changes how we think, speak, live, and love. It is visible not just in our church attendance or theology, but in the very shape of our lives.

Jesus never invited people to simply believe in the Kingdom—He called them to live under its rule.

So, what does that look like?

This chapter explores the distinct marks of someone who lives not as a refugee of the world, but as a full citizen of the Kingdom of God.

1. Allegiance to the King

At the heart of Kingdom citizenship is loyalty to Jesus Christ. He is not just Savior—He is Lord. *"Why do you call me, 'Lord, Lord,' and do not do what I say?" (Luke 6:46)*

A Kingdom citizen does not live according to the culture, trends, or politics of the day, but by the Word of the King. This allegiance affects every decision—how we spend our time, use our money, treat others, and pursue justice.

Question: Is Christ the true King of your daily life?

2. A Life of Repentance and Renewal

Kingdom citizens are not perfect—but they are being perfected.

They don't excuse sin—they confess it. They don't stay stagnant—they grow. They are shaped by repentance, not rebellion; by renewal, not routine. *"Be transformed by the renewing of your mind…" (Romans 12:2)*

This means allowing God to reshape your thoughts, desires, and habits so that your life reflects the values of His Kingdom.

3. The Fruit of the Spirit

Jesus said, *"By their fruit you will recognize them" (Matthew 7:16)*. The evidence of Kingdom citizenship is not titles or positions, but transformed character.

Paul describes the fruit of a Spirit-led life: *"Love, joy, peace, patience, kindness, goodness, faithfulness, gentleness, and self-control..." (Galatians 5:22–23)*

These qualities are not personality traits—they are spiritual fruit. They grow in us as we stay rooted in Christ and surrender to His work within us.

A refugee lives by fear. A citizen lives by fruit.

4. Love for the Body of Christ

Kingdom citizens are not lone wolves—they are part of a people. *"You are a chosen race, a royal priesthood, a holy nation, a people for His own possession..." (1 Peter 2:9)*

Citizens of heaven are deeply committed to the Church—not as an institution, but as a family. They worship together, serve one another, bear each other's burdens, and walk in unity.

Loving the Church is not optional. Jesus died for her. And those who love the King will love His bride.

5. A Witness to the World

Kingdom citizens do not blend in—they stand out. Jesus said, *"You are the light of the world. A city on a hill cannot be hidden" (Matthew 5:14).* Citizenship comes with a mission: to reflect the goodness, truth, and beauty of the King in a dark world.

This happens through:
- Integrity in the workplace
- Compassion in our communities
- Boldness in evangelism
- Mercy in conflict
- Justice for the oppressed
- Humility in leadership

Your life is meant to be a signpost—pointing others to the reality of God's Kingdom.

6. Unshakable Hope

Earthly kingdoms rise and fall. The economy fluctuates. Leaders disappoint. Circumstances change. But Kingdom citizens are anchored in a hope that cannot be shaken. *"Since we are receiving a Kingdom that cannot be shaken, let us be thankful..." (Hebrews 12:28)*

This hope isn't naïve. It's rooted in the resurrection of Christ and the promise of His return. It enables Kingdom citizens to face suffering with confidence, endure trials with peace, and live sacrificially without fear.

7. A Cross-Carrying Life

Jesus made it clear: *"Whoever wants to be my disciple must deny themselves and take up their cross daily and follow me." (Luke 9:23)*

Kingdom citizenship is costly. It requires sacrifice, obedience, and sometimes rejection by the world. But it is worth it—for in losing our lives, we find them.

A citizen lives not for self, but for the glory of God and the good of others. The cross is not just a symbol—it is a way of life.

REFLECTION:
- Which of these marks do you see most clearly in your life?

- Which ones do you struggle with?

- What is one step you can take to grow more fully into your Kingdom citizenship?

The Kingdom of God is not a theory. It is a reality that reshapes lives. If you belong to Christ, you are not a refugee looking for a place to belong. You are a citizen with a divine passport, a heavenly mission, and a new identity.

Let your life reflect the Kingdom you now belong to—so that others, still wandering, may find their way home through you.

*In the next chapter, we'll explore the powerful transition **from estranged to engrafted**—how God brings outsiders into His family and turns spiritual wanderers into heirs of the Kingdom.*

Chapter 6

FROM ESTRANGED TO ENGRAFTED

"Once you were not a people, but now you are the people of God; once you had not received mercy, but now you have received mercy." —1 Peter 2:10 (NIV)

One of the most beautiful truths of the Gospel is that God takes the **estranged, the outcast, and the outsider,** and brings them near. He does not simply forgive sin—He **restores relationship**. He does not merely invite us to visit the Kingdom—He **engrafts us into the family tree** and birthed into the church community

This chapter is a celebration of the **transforming power of divine inclusion**—how God takes spiritual refugees and makes them permanent citizens.

1. Estranged: Once Far Off

Before Christ, we were all spiritual refugees—cut off from God, without a true home. Paul writes of this condition: *"Remember that at that time you were separate from Christ... foreigners to the covenants of the promise, without hope and without God in the world."* —Ephesians 2:12 (NIV)

Estrangement means:

- No covenant relationship
- No legal claim to the promises of God
- No access to God's presence
- Living as spiritual outsiders

Many today still carry this estrangement in their hearts—even in the Church. They may know about God but feel distant, unworthy, or uninvited. But God never leaves us in this state.

2. Engrafted: Brought Near by Grace

Through Christ, everything changes. *"But now in Christ Jesus you who once were far away have been brought near by the blood of Christ."* —Ephesians 2:13 (NIV)

God does not just forgive; He **brings us near**. He makes us part of His household, His people, and His family. This is more than adoption—it's **engraftment**.

Paul uses the image of an olive tree in Romans 11:

- The natural branches represent Israel.
- The wild branches (Gentiles) are grafted in.
- Together, they draw life from the same root: **Christ.**

"You, though a wild olive shoot, have been grafted in among the others and now share in the nourishing sap from the olive root." —Romans 11:17 (NIV)

This is not symbolic—it is a **spiritual reality**. You now:

- Share in the inheritance of the saints
- Receive the same Spirit
- Have the same access to the Father
- Are equally loved, chosen, and commissioned

3. The Power of Engraftment

To be **engrafted** is to be:
- **Connected** – no longer spiritually homeless
- **Sustained** – nourished by divine life
- **Productive** – bearing fruit for the Kingdom
- **Secure** – held by God, not by works

You are not an add-on or a guest. You are not second-tier or temporary. You are part of **God's original plan**. Your citizenship is legitimate, eternal, and unshakable.

"He predestined us for adoption to sonship through Jesus Christ, in accordance with his pleasure and will." —Ephesians 1:5 (NIV)

4. Let Go of the Refugee Mentality

When God brings you near, you must **renew your mindset**. Many believers have been legally engrafted, but mentally still live as outsiders. They doubt:

- That they truly belong
- That God is fully pleased with them
- That they can walk in Kingdom authority

But just as a branch does not graft itself, neither do we earn our place in Christ. It is a work of **grace**, sealed by the Holy Spirit.

"You also were included in Christ... when you believed, you were marked in him with a seal, the promised Holy Spirit." —Ephesians 1:13 (NIV)

5. Living as the People of God

Once estranged, we are now called:
- A chosen generation
- A royal priesthood
- A holy nation
- God's special possession (1 Peter 2:9)

We have purpose, identity, and belonging. We are called to **declare His praises** and **demonstrate His reign**.

NO LONGER WANDERING—YOU ARE HOME.

Refugees hope for a place to belong. Citizens know they are home. In Christ, you are:

- Forgiven
- Accepted
- Planted
- Engrafted
- Empowered

The journey from spiritual refugee to Kingdom citizen is not meant to be walked alone. God never intended for His people to be isolated individuals. From the beginning, He has been forming a people, a family, a community—a visible expression of His invisible Kingdom.

That community is the Church.

Too often, people view the Church as an institution, an event, or a building. But in the Kingdom of God, the Church is much more than that. It is the living, breathing, gathered community of citizens who have been called out of exile into God's marvelous light (1 Peter 2:9).

In this chapter, we will explore what it means to be part of the Church as a Kingdom community—not just as attendees or members, but as engaged citizens in a holy nation.

1. The Church Is the Embassy of the Kingdom

An embassy is a place where the values and laws of one nation are represented in the land of another. That's what the Church is: an embassy of heaven on earth.

Jesus said, *"You are the light of the world. A city on a hill cannot be hidden." (Matthew 5:14)*

When the Church gathers, it is a glimpse of the coming Kingdom. It's where:

- The King is worshipped.
- The citizens are equipped.
- The broken are restored.
- The mission is reinforced.

The Church is not the Kingdom in its fullness, but it is evidence that the Kingdom has come and is coming.

2. A Family for Former Refugees

Many people arrive in church wounded, disconnected, and spiritually homeless. But in the Church, they find not only forgiveness, but belonging. *"You are no longer foreigners and strangers, but fellow citizens with God's people and members of His household." (Ephesians 2:19)*

The Church is meant to be:
- A place where spiritual refugees become citizens.
- A table where outsiders become family.
- A community where no one stands alone.

When the Church functions as the Kingdom community God intended, it becomes a home for the homeless and a beacon for the broken.

3. Marked by Love and Unity

Jesus gave His followers a new command: *"Love one another. As I have loved you, so you must love one another. By this everyone will know that you are my disciples..." (John 13:34–35)*

Love is the primary mark of Kingdom community. Not programs. Not buildings. Not impressive services. Love.

Unity doesn't mean sameness—it means oneness in Christ. The Church is made up of diverse people, backgrounds, and gifts, but all are united under one Lord, one faith, and one Spirit.

When we love and serve each other well, the Church becomes a witness to the world of what life in God's Kingdom looks like.

4. Equipped for Mission

The Church is not just a safe haven—it is a training ground. *"Christ himself gave the apostles, the prophets, the evangelists, the pastors and teachers, to equip his people for works of service..." (Ephesians 4:11–12)*

Citizens of the Kingdom are not called to be spectators, but participants. The Church exists to:

- Equip the saints for ministry.
- Send out missionaries into neighbourhoods and nations.
- Train disciples who make disciples.
- Support the weary, challenge the complacent, and encourage the faithful.

A Kingdom citizen sees the Church not as a consumer, but as a contributor—bringing their gifts, energy, and love to the shared mission of God.

5. A Place of Accountability and Growth

Kingdom community means we walk with others who help us stay aligned with the King. *"Let us consider how we may spur one another on toward love and good deeds..." (Hebrews 10:24)*

The Church is where:
- Sin is confronted in love.
- Truth is spoken in grace.
- Restoration is pursued with humility.
- Growth happens in relationship, not isolation.

Accountability is not about control—it's about care. In a healthy Church, we don't let each other drift. We walk together, confess together, and grow together.

6. A Preview of What Is to Come

The Church is a present community with a future promise. *"Let us rejoice and be glad and give him glory! For the wedding of the Lamb has come, and his bride has made herself ready."* (Revelation 19:7)

The Church is the bride of Christ, being prepared for her Bridegroom. One day, Jesus will return, and the Kingdom will come in fullness. Until then, the Church lives in anticipation—pointing forward to that day through worship, holiness, and mission.

Every time the Church gathers, forgives, serves, and loves, it whispers to the world:

"This is what eternity will be like."

REFLECTION:

- How do you view the Church: as a consumer or as a citizen?
- Are you actively contributing to the mission and life of your local church?
- In what ways can you reflect the love and unity of the Kingdom in your church community?

The Church is not perfect, but it is God's chosen community for Kingdom citizens. It is the place where spiritual exiles become sons and daughters, where the lonely find family, and where the broken are restored.

If you are a citizen of heaven, the Church is not optional—it is essential. So, show up. Serve well. Love deeply. Forgive freely. Worship boldly.

---

*In the next chapter, we'll address a vital issue: the difference between **religion and true faith**, and how many people live as **refugees by religion**, not relationship.*

Chapter 7

REFUGEES BY RELIGION, NOT BY FAITH

"They have a form of godliness but deny its power."
—2 Timothy 3:5 (NIV)

Religion can give us rituals, rules, and routines—but only **faith** gives us relationship, righteousness, and rest. There is a tragic reality in the Church today: many people live as **spiritual refugees**, not because they are far from church, but because they are far from Christ. They are close to **religion**, but distant from **faith**.

This chapter is a call to discern the difference between **religious performance** and **Kingdom**

citizenship, and to examine our hearts honestly in light of the Gospel.

1. Religion Creates Refugees

Religion—without the Spirit and truth of Christ—can leave people:

- Overburdened
- Spiritually homeless
- Emotionally exhausted
- Disconnected from the heart of God

Jesus rebuked the religious leaders of His day, not because of their zeal, but because of their **hypocrisy and hardness**.

"Woe to you, teachers of the law and Pharisees, you hypocrites! You shut the door of the kingdom of heaven in people's faces." —Matthew 23:13 (NIV)

They maintained **a system** but missed **the Saviour**. They had the scrolls, the synagogues, and the sacrifices, but not the **spirit of sonship**. Religion built walls—faith builds bridges.

2. Symptoms of Religious Refugees

Some believers wear the uniform of Christianity but live like orphans:

- They serve out of fear, not love
- They perform to earn favour, not from identity
- They hide weakness behind spiritual language
- They are never at rest, always striving

This creates anxiety, shame, and burnout. It leaves people active in ministry but empty in soul.

"Come to me, all you who are weary and burdened, and I will give you rest." —Matthew 11:28 (NIV)

Jesus did not come to start a new religion—He came to offer **relationship** with the Father.

3. The Elder Brother Syndrome

The parable of the prodigal son (Luke 15) reveals two sons:

- The younger son rebelled and returned.
- The older son stayed home but was **just as lost**.

Though physically present, the elder brother lived with a **refugee heart**:

- He felt like a servant, not a son.
- He resented the Father's grace toward others.
- He obeyed without joy or intimacy.

"All these years I've been slaving for you and never disobeyed your orders..." —Luke 15:29 (NIV)

Many churchgoers today are elder brothers. They are busy for God but bitter inside. They need to rediscover **grace**, not grind.

4. Faith Brings Belonging

True faith in Christ doesn't just change our theology—it transforms our identity. Through faith:

- We are made **righteous**, not just religious.
- We become **sons and daughters**, not servants under fear.
- We walk in **liberty**, not legalism.

"For in Christ Jesus you are all children of God through faith." —Galatians 3:26 (NIV)

Faith brings us to rest. It silences the inner critic. It opens the door to intimacy with the Father. It delivers us from both sin **and self-righteousness**.

5. The Danger of a Religious Refugee Spirit

When someone stays in the system of religion without genuine faith:

- They may burn out without bearing fruit.
- They become critical, not compassionate.
- They begin to compare, not celebrate.
- They lose joy, power, and peace.

They may look like citizens, but live like captives. They need an encounter with the living Christ—not just the machinery of ministry.

6. Return to the Heart of the Father

Whether you've run far away like the prodigal, or stayed close but cold like the elder brother, the Father's arms are open.

"My son... everything I have is yours." —Luke 15:31 (NIV)

You don't have to live outside the house or inside with bitterness. You can enter the **joy of sonship**, the rest of relationship, and the fullness of Kingdom life.

Religion may give you a place to serve—but only Christ gives you a place to **belong**.

---

*In the next chapter, we will shift from identity to authority and explore what it means to **walk in Kingdom authority** as a citizen—not just with belief, but with boldness.*

Chapter 8
WALKING IN KINGDOM AUTHORITY

"I have given you authority... to overcome all the power of the enemy; nothing will harm you." —
Luke 10:19 (NIV)

Many believers know they are forgiven. Fewer know they are **empowered**. Salvation is not only about being rescued—it is also about being **commissioned**. As citizens of the Kingdom of God, we have not just been brought near; we have been **sent out**—with power, purpose, and **authority**.

This chapter explores the incredible truth that Kingdom citizenship carries Kingdom

responsibility and dominion. We are not passive spectators in God's plan. We are **participants**, clothed in His authority, and called to extend His rule on earth.

Being a citizen of the Kingdom of God does not remove us from the world—it sends us into it. While our allegiance is to heaven, our address remains on earth. We are Kingdom people living in a land that often opposes our King.

This tension is not accidental—it is intentional. *"But our citizenship is in heaven. And we eagerly await a Savior from there, the Lord Jesus Christ." (Philippians 3:20)*

As citizens of heaven, we are called to live differently—faithfully, humbly, courageously—in the midst of a world that does not yet recognize our King.

This chapter explores what it means to live faithfully as a Kingdom citizen in a foreign land.

1. Ambassadors, Not Escape Artists

Jesus didn't save us to hide us from the world. He prayed: *"My prayer is not that you take them out of the world but that you protect them from the evil one." (John 17:15)*

Kingdom citizens are not called to escape culture but to engage it—not to conform to the world, but to represent another world.

We are ambassadors (2 Corinthians 5:20)—God's representatives on foreign soil. We live and speak on behalf of the King. This includes:

- Bringing truth where there is confusion.
- Offering hope where there is despair.
- Practicing holiness in the midst of compromise.
- Loving enemies in a culture of division.

You are not here by accident. You've been sent.

2. Exiles with Purpose

Peter calls believers "foreigners and exiles" (1 Peter 2:11). The early Church understood they were resident aliens—in the world, but not of it.

They didn't try to blend in. But they also didn't withdraw. Instead, they lived with integrity, generosity, and boldness—so much so that people "praised God" because of them (1 Peter 2:12).

As modern-day exiles, we are not aimless—we are on assignment. Every neighbourhood, workplace and nation is a place where Kingdom citizens can shine.

The question is: Will we live as refugees, retreating from the world, or as citizens, reclaiming it for the King?

3. Living by Kingdom Values

The world has its own values—success, self-interest, status, comfort. But the Kingdom flips those, upside down:

- The first shall be last.
- The meek shall inherit the earth.
- Blessed are the poor in spirit.
- Love your enemies.

These aren't slogans. They are marching orders for citizens of heaven.

Living by Kingdom values means choosing:

- Humility over pride
- Purity over compromise
- Generosity over greed
- Service over selfishness
- Truth over convenience

This kind of life will often look foolish to the world—but it is the wisdom of God.

4. Facing Hostility with Grace

Jesus warned that Kingdom living would come at a cost: *"If the world hates you, keep in mind that it hated me first." (John 15:18)*

Being a citizen in a foreign land means you may face:

- Rejection for your faith
- Pressure to conform
- Misunderstanding or mockery
- Temptation to compromise

But Jesus also promised blessing: *"Blessed are those who are persecuted because of righteousness, for theirs is the Kingdom of heaven."* (Matthew 5:10)

We are called to respond not with fear or aggression, but with grace, courage, and love. Our goal is not to win arguments but to win hearts — to reflect the King even in conflict.

5. Living with Holy Distinction

In a foreign land, citizens of the Kingdom are meant to stand out — not for attention, but for testimony. *"Do not conform to the pattern of this world, but be transformed…"* (Romans 12:2)

This means:

- Your ethics are different.
- Your speech is different.
- Your entertainment choices, financial decisions, and relationships are different —

not legalistically, but out of loyalty to your King.

When people notice your distinctiveness, it creates space for witness. It invites curiosity. It opens hearts to the reality of a better Kingdom.

6. Longing for Home, Labouring in the Field

Every Kingdom citizen carries a deep homesickness—a longing for the day when Jesus returns and the Kingdom is revealed in full.

But that longing doesn't lead us to apathy—it fuels our mission. *"Therefore, my dear brothers and sisters, stand firm. Let nothing move you. Always give yourselves fully to the work of the Lord..."* (1 Corinthians 15:58)

Until the King returns, we keep building, loving, preaching, and serving. We're not tourists waiting for our ride—we're workers preparing the way.

1. What Is Kingdom Authority?

Authority is **delegated power**. It is the right to act, speak, and command—not in your own name, but in the name of another. Jesus, as the King of Kings, possesses **all authority**:

"All authority in heaven and on earth has been given to me." —Matthew 28:18 (NIV)

And then He delegated that authority to us: *"Therefore, go and make disciples..."* —Matthew 28:19 (NIV)

Kingdom authority is not about controlling people—it is about:
- Advancing God's will
- Destroying works of darkness
- Setting captives free
- Manifesting the Kingdom on earth

2. Authority Is Given to Citizens, Not Visitors.

Only those who **belong** can represent the King. Spiritual refugees may know the promises, but lack the posture to carry Kingdom power.

Authority comes to those who are:
- Under submission to Christ
- Walking in righteousness
- Rooted in spiritual identity
- Filled with the Holy Spirit

"Submit yourselves, then, to God. Resist the devil, and he will flee from you." —James 4:7 (NIV)

Submission unlocks resistance. You cannot exercise authority **over darkness** if you are not submitted **under the Light**.

3. Examples of Kingdom Authority in Action

Kingdom authority is not abstract—it is real and practical. It's visible in the early Church:

- **Healing the sick**: *"In the name of Jesus Christ of Nazareth, walk."* (Acts 3:6)
- **Casting out demons**: *"In the name of Jesus Christ, I command you to come out."* (Acts 16:18)
- **Bold proclamation**: *"We must obey God rather than human beings!"* (Acts 5:29)

Kingdom citizens speak **with Heaven's backing**. Their words carry weight. Their presence brings change. Their prayers shift atmospheres.

4. Walking in Personal Authority

Every believer can walk in authority over:

- **Sin** – You are no longer a slave (Romans 6:14)
- **Fear** – You've received a Spirit of power (2 Timothy 1:7)
- **Temptation** – God provides a way out (1 Corinthians 10:13)
- **Demonic opposition** – You overcome by the blood and testimony (Revelation 12:11)

But you must **believe** and **exercise** what has been given.

"The one who believes in me will do the works I have been doing, and they will do even greater things..."
—John 14:12 (NIV)

5. The Dangers of Neglecting Authority

Some believers live far below their spiritual capacity because:

- They fear stepping out
- They doubt their worth
- They are unaware of what Christ has made available

The enemy thrives on ignorance. If he can convince you that you're powerless, you'll never confront him. But when you realise your authority, you will no longer accept defeat, delay, or deception.

"My people are destroyed from lack of knowledge."
—Hosea 4:6 (NIV)

6. Authority Flows from Identity

You don't need a title to carry authority—you need identity. Jesus didn't say, "These signs will follow apostles or pastors." He said: *"These signs will accompany those who believe..."* —Mark 16:17 (NIV)

Authority doesn't come from performance, but from **position in Christ**. If you know who you are, and whose you are, you can walk boldly into any environment and declare, *"The Kingdom of God is here!"*

7. Authority Must Be Exercised in Love and Humility

Kingdom authority is never about control, manipulation, or personal glory. It is:

- Rooted in love
- Expressed through service
- Submitted to Christ
- Confirmed by fruit

Jesus washed feet—even though He held all authority in Heaven and earth. True power is best expressed through **servanthood**.

YOU ARE AN AMBASSADOR

You don't just represent a denomination—you represent **a Kingdom**. You are not a refugee hoping for crumbs—you are an **ambassador empowered with keys** (Matthew 16:19).

Use them.

REFLECTION:

- Where are you tempted to blend in instead of stand out as a Kingdom citizen?
- How can you live more intentionally as an ambassador for Christ in your current context?
- What "foreign land" has God placed you in, and how can you bring His Kingdom there?

To live as a citizen in a foreign land is not easy—but it is worth it. The world may not understand your allegiance, but the King sees every act of faithfulness. Your citizenship is not just a title—it is your identity, your calling, and your witness.

So, walk boldly. Speak truthfully. Love deeply. And remember: You may feel out of place here—but you are not lost. You are a citizen of a Kingdom that cannot be shaken. And one day soon, the King will return to take you home.

*In the next chapter, we'll look at how Kingdom citizens not only carry authority, but also **live out Kingdom culture**—displaying Heaven's values, conduct, and influence in a broken world.*

Chapter 9

KINGDOM CULTURE AND CITIZENSHIP CONDUCT

"But seek first his kingdom and his righteousness, and all these things will be given to you as well." — *Matthew 6:33 (NIV)*

Every kingdom has a culture. It carries customs, values, language, laws, and a way of life that distinguishes it from others. The Kingdom of God is no different. It is **not just a place—it is a way of living.** Kingdom citizenship means **adopting Kingdom culture.**

This chapter examines what it means to live as a **citizen of the Kingdom** in a world that often promotes opposite values. We will explore what the **conduct of a Kingdom citizen** looks like, how it contrasts with worldly systems, and how it brings transformation to every area of life.

1. Kingdom Culture Comes from the King

Culture flows from leadership. In the Kingdom of God, the character of the King defines the character of the Kingdom.

Jesus is:

- Humble
- Holy
- Compassionate
- Truthful
- Just
- Loving

Therefore, His Kingdom culture reflects:

- **Holiness** over compromise
- **Humility** over pride
- **Love** over hatred
- **Grace** over law
- **Truth** over deception

- **Peace** over anxiety

"The kingdom of God is not a matter of eating and drinking, but of righteousness, peace and joy in the Holy Spirit." —Romans 14:17 (NIV)

2. The Beatitudes: A Kingdom Manifesto

In Matthew 5, Jesus gave a clear blueprint for Kingdom character:

- *"Blessed are the poor in spirit…"*
- *"Blessed are the meek…"*
- *"Blessed are the merciful…"*
- *"Blessed are those who hunger and thirst for righteousness…"*

These statements describe the **internal posture** and **external lifestyle** of those who belong to the Kingdom. They are not suggestions—they are descriptions of true citizens.

3. The Conduct of a Kingdom Citizen

Kingdom citizenship is not just theological—it is **practical**. It affects how you:

- Treat others
- Handle money
- Respond to offense
- Speak and think
- View power and success

Key traits of Kingdom conduct include:

a. Love Your Enemies

"Love your enemies and pray for those who persecute you." —Matthew 5:44 (NIV). Kingdom love goes beyond what is deserved. It reflects the mercy of God.

b. Forgive Quickly

"Forgive, and you will be forgiven." —Luke 6:37 (NIV). Forgiveness is not optional—it is a Kingdom mandate. Citizens carry no grudges.

c. Pursue Righteousness

"Be holy, because I am holy." —1 Peter 1:16 (NIV). Kingdom citizens pursue personal holiness and integrity.

d. Honour Others

"Be devoted to one another in love. Honour one another above yourselves." —Romans 12:10 (NIV). Citizens build a culture of honour in word, attitude, and relationships.

e. Serve Selflessly

"Whoever wants to become great among you must be your servant." —Matthew 20:26 (NIV) Greatness in the Kingdom comes through servanthood.

4. Kingdom Culture vs. World Culture

World Culture	Kingdom Culture
Pride	Humility
Greed	Generosity
Lust	Purity
Self-promotion	Servanthood
Retaliation	Forgiveness
Competition	Unity
Fear	Faith

Citizens of the Kingdom live **counterculturally**. They do not conform to the pattern of the world, but are transformed by the renewing of their minds (Romans 12:2).

5. Kingdom Influence in Daily Life

Kingdom culture is not limited to Sunday—it invades:

- **Homes** – with peace, love, and honour
- **Workplaces** – with excellence, integrity, and witness
- **Schools and campuses** – with courage and truth
- **Communities** – through justice, service, and compassion

Jesus said: *"You are the salt of the earth... You are the light of the world."* —Matthew 5:13–14 (NIV)

Salt preserves. Light reveals. Kingdom citizens influence the environment around them. They don't hide—they shine.

6. Empowered by the Spirit

We cannot live out Kingdom culture by sheer effort. It is the work of the **Holy Spirit** within us that transforms our nature and empowers our conduct.

"Live by the Spirit, and you will not gratify the desires of the flesh." —Galatians 5:16 (NIV)

When we walk with the Spirit, the fruit of the Spirit flows:

- Love, joy, peace
- Patience, kindness, goodness
- Faithfulness, gentleness, self-control

This is the culture of Heaven made visible on earth. You Are a Walking Embassy. Every Kingdom citizen is an **ambassador**, carrying the culture of Heaven into the earth. People should encounter you and **taste the values of another realm**.

"As he is, so are we in this world." —1 John 4:17

*In the next chapter, we will look at one of Jesus' most powerful Kingdom parables—**the prodigal son**—and what it teaches us about coming home to the Father and rediscovering our citizenship.*

Chapter 10

RETURNING HOME: THE PRODIGAL AND THE KINGDOM

"But while he was still a long way off, his father saw him and was filled with compassion for him; he ran to his son, threw his arms around him and kissed him." —Luke 15:20 (NIV)

The parable of the prodigal son is one of the most powerful illustrations of God's Kingdom heart. It is not merely a story about rebellion—it is a story about identity, citizenship, and restoration.

This chapter reveals that Kingdom citizenship can be lost in the mind before it is ever lost in action. But no matter how far someone has wandered, the Father's arms remain open to receive, restore, and re-establish them as sons.

1. A Citizen Who Chose Refugee Life

The younger son began in the Father's house, with all the rights of a son. He had identity, inheritance, and intimacy. But he made a decision: *"Father, give me my share of the estate." (Luke 15:12, NIV)*

This was more than financial rebellion—it was relational severance. He wanted the benefits of the Kingdom without the boundaries of the King.

So, he:

- Left his place
- Spent his inheritance
- Lost his dignity
- Found himself in a far-off land

He was still a son by birth, but he had chosen the life of a refugee—disconnected, desperate, and dishonoured.

2. Wilderness Brings Clarity

In the pigpen of life, stripped of resources and reputation, the prodigal came to his senses: *"How many of my father's hired servants have food to spare, and here I am starving to death!"* —Luke 15:17 (NIV)

Refugee living will eventually confront us with our need for home, identity, and relationship. The turning point is not when we clean ourselves up—but when we remember where we belong. The prodigal said: *"I will set out and go back to my father..."* (v. 18)

This is the beginning of repentance—not just feeling guilty but changing direction.

3. The Heart of the Father

What sets this story apart is the scandalous grace of the Father:

- He sees the son "a long way off"
- He runs—something no dignified man in that culture would do

- He embraces the broken boy
- He restores him with robe, ring, and shoes

"For this son of mine was dead and is alive again; he was lost and is found."
—*Luke 15:24 (NIV)*

The Father never called him a slave. He never required him to earn his way back. He restored his status, intimacy, and authority—not because of the son's goodness, but because of the Father's love.

This is Kingdom grace. It does not rehabilitate the refugee—it reinstates the citizen.

4. Lessons from the Elder Brother

The elder brother had never left home, yet was also distant in heart. He refused to celebrate his brother's return.

"Look! All these years I've been slaving for you..."
(Luke 15:29, NIV)

This mindset reveals:

- A religious spirit
- A servant mentality, not sonship
- Resentment toward grace

The Father's response is telling: *"My son... everything I have is yours."* —Luke 15:31 (NIV)

Many Christians live in the house of God yet don't feel at home. They serve faithfully but have never embraced their full identity. They are citizens by position but refugees in mindset.

5. Coming Home to the Kingdom

Whether you are a prodigal in the pigpen or a bitter brother in the field, the invitation is the same: Come home.

God is not interested in your religious record. He is interested in relationship. He wants you:

- In His presence
- At His table
- Wearing your robe of righteousness
- Walking in sonship, not survival

"He brought me out into a spacious place; he rescued me because he delighted in me." —Psalm 18:19 (NIV)

6. Restore the Ring

The ring in the parable symbolises authority and identity. God wants to put His ring back on your finger:

- The authority to pray
- The authority to forgive
- The authority to declare His Word
- The authority to walk as His representative

It's time to stop living beneath your calling. You are not a refugee—you are a royal citizen.

In the next chapter, we'll step back and look at the bigger picture: how the global Church is meant to function as a community of Kingdom citizens, not just religious spectators.

Chapter 11

THE GLOBAL CHURCH: A COMMUNITY OF CITIZENS

"Consequently, you are no longer foreigners and strangers, but fellow citizens with God's people and also members of his household." —Ephesians 2:19

The Church is not just a religious institution—it is the visible expression of **the Kingdom of God on earth**. It is not just a congregation of believers, but a **community of citizens**, called to live out the values, authority, and culture of Heaven. While the Kingdom is eternal and spiritual, the Church is the **body of citizens gathered**, acting as an embassy of that Kingdom in every nation, tribe, and tongue.

This chapter reveals the corporate nature of Kingdom citizenship and challenges us to view the Church not merely as a place we attend, but as a **citizen collective on a Kingdom mission.**

1. One Kingdom, One Church, Many Nations

The Kingdom of God transcends all man-made borders and divisions. It is not limited to:

- Nationality
- Race
- Denomination
- Geography

"There is neither Jew nor Gentile... for you are all one in Christ Jesus." —Galatians 3:28 (NIV)

From every corner of the globe, God is calling people into His Kingdom—and uniting them into **one global Church.**

"You have made them to be a kingdom and priests to serve our God, and they will reign on the earth." — Revelation 5:10 (NIV)

The Church is the **visible assembly** of Kingdom citizens, living together under one King.

2. The Church Is a Colony of Heaven

Paul reminds the Philippians that their **citizenship is in Heaven** (Philippians 3:20). That means the Church is a **colony of Heaven** in the midst of the earth—bringing Heaven's values to earth's systems.

This means:

- We reflect God's culture in our community
- We carry God's justice in our cities
- We speak Heaven's truth in earthly confusion
- We are **in the world, but not of it**

The Church is not just a place for teaching and singing—it is a **Kingdom training ground** for citizens who are called to impact the world.

3. The Church Must Disciple Citizens, Not Just Entertain Guests

Too many churches today aim to attract attenders, not to **disciple citizens**. The result is crowds who are informed but not transformed.

True Kingdom churches:

- Preach repentance and grace
- Teach identity and obedience
- Activate gifts and callings
- Send believers as ambassadors

"Go and make disciples of all nations..." —Matthew 28:19 (NIV)

Discipleship is the **citizenship process** of the Kingdom. It moves people from believing to becoming—from attendance to assignment.

4. Citizenship Comes with Responsibility

In earthly nations, citizens have both **rights** and **responsibilities**. The same is true in the Kingdom:

- **Right** to access God's presence → **Responsibility** to represent His nature
- **Right** to pray and receive → **Responsibility** to serve and give
- **Right** to be fed → **Responsibility** to feed others
- **Right** to freedom in Christ → **Responsibility** to use freedom to build, not destroy

The Church is healthiest when every citizen plays their part. *"From him the whole body... grows and builds itself up in love, as each part does its work."* —Ephesians 4:16 (NIV)

5. A Unified Church Reflects a United Kingdom

Division among believers undermines the message of the Kingdom. Jesus prayed for unity, not uniformity. *"That all of them may be one, Father... so that the world may believe that you have sent me."* —John 17:21 (NIV)

Unity among Kingdom citizens:

- Releases anointing (Psalm 133)
- Displays God's glory
- Attracts the lost
- Multiplies effectiveness

The Church must model **Kingdom unity in diversity**—celebrating differences while remaining committed to the same King and mission.

6. The Church Must Challenge Refugee Thinking

The Church is called to:

- Welcome the wandering
- Heal the broken
- Teach the confused
- Establish the estranged
- Empower the insecure

We must help believers move from mere **membership** to full **citizenship**. We must teach people not just how to attend services, but how to **live under the rule of Christ**.

7. The Global Church Is God's Embassy

In the natural world, an embassy is:

- A sovereign representation of a kingdom in a foreign land
- A place of refuge, safety, and authority
- Staffed by citizens and led by ambassadors

So it is with the Church:

- We represent Heaven on earth
- We are a safe place for the broken
- We carry legal and spiritual authority
- We are led by Christ, the King, through His Spirit

Every local church is an **embassy of Heaven**, filled with **citizens, not visitors**.

8. Let the Church Be the Church

It's time for the Church to recover her identity:

- Not just a community centre, but a **Kingdom centre**

- Not just a place for crowds, but a **place for citizens**
- Not just a stage for performers, but a **training ground for ambassadors**

The world doesn't need another club or concert. It needs a **citizen-led, Spirit-filled, Christ-centred Church** that lives and loves as Heaven does.

Chapter 12

THE COST AND REWARD OF KINGDOM CITIZENSHIP

Following Jesus is free—but it will cost you everything. This paradox lies at the heart of the Gospel. The grace of God cannot be earned or bought, yet true Kingdom citizenship demands a surrender of all we are and all we have. Jesus never minimized this. He invited people to come, but also warned them to count the cost.

"Whoever does not carry their cross and follow me cannot be my disciple." (Luke 14:27)

The Kingdom of God is not for the half-hearted. It is for those who are willing to leave behind the old world to embrace a new one—who let go of their refugee status to fully step into their role as citizens of heaven.

This chapter explores the real cost and the eternal reward of being a citizen of God's Kingdom.

1. Counting the Cost

In Luke 14, Jesus gives a strong warning about what it means to follow Him. He compares it to building a tower or going to war—serious endeavours that require intentional preparation. *"Suppose one of you wants to build a tower. Won't you first sit down and estimate the cost..."* (Luke 14:28)

To be a citizen of the Kingdom means:

- Saying no to self-centeredness.
- Turning from sin and comfort.
- Being willing to be misunderstood or rejected.
- Living under the Lordship of Christ, not your own preferences.

This is not a casual membership. It is a lifetime allegiance.

2. Surrendering Your Refugee Identity

There is a strange comfort in spiritual exile. Some people prefer wandering to commitment. But the call of Jesus is clear: *"Whoever wants to save their life will lose it, but whoever loses their life for me will find it."* (Matthew 16:25)

You cannot cling to the identity of a refugee—fearful, uncommitted, self-preserving—and expect to live as a bold, free Kingdom citizen.

True citizenship requires letting go:

- Of bitterness and unforgiveness
- Of worldly ambition and control
- Of the need to be accepted by everyone
- Of the illusion that you are your own master

Only when you surrender all can Christ truly reign in your life.

3. The Hidden Rewards Now

While the full reward of citizenship is eternal, there are blessings now for those who live under Christ's rule:

- Peace that surpasses understanding (Philippians 4:7)
- Joy that is not tied to circumstances (John 15:11)
- Purpose greater than success or survival (Ephesians 2:10)
- Community that reflects God's love (Acts 2:42–47)
- Power to live differently (Romans 8:11)

These are not rewards the world can give. They are signs of God's presence in the life of a citizen who has made the King their everything.

4. The Eternal Reward Later

Paul wrote: *"I consider that our present sufferings are not worth comparing with the glory that will be revealed in us." (Romans 8:18)*

The reward of Kingdom citizenship is not just peace in this life—it is glory in the next.

Jesus promised:

- A crown of righteousness (2 Timothy 4:8)

- A place prepared in His Father's house (John 14:2–3)

- Eternal life in a world made new (Revelation 21:1–5)

The refugee seeks temporary shelter. The citizen receives an eternal home.

5. Living in Light of the Reward

Hebrews 11 describes men and women of faith who lived as strangers on the earth. Why? Because *"they were looking for a better country—a heavenly one" (Hebrews 11:16).*

Citizens of the Kingdom live with the end in mind. They understand that:

- Suffering is temporary.

- Earthly rewards are fleeting.

- Faithfulness now will be honoured then.

- The King will return, and His justice will reign.

We can endure hardship, say no to sin, and serve with joy because we know what's coming.

6. No Regrets in the Kingdom

Some fear that if they give up too much for Jesus, they will miss out on life. But no one who has truly surrendered to Christ has ever looked back and said, "I gave too much."

Instead, they say:

- "I gained more than I lost."
- "I found life when I gave mine up."
- "He was worth it all."

"No one who has left home or brothers or sisters or mother or father or children or fields for me and the gospel will fail to receive a hundred times as much…" (Mark 10:29–30)

To lose your life for Christ is to find it. To surrender all to the Kingdom is to gain everything that matters.

REFLECTION:

- Have you truly counted the cost of following Jesus?
- Is there anything you're still clinging to that hinders your full citizenship?
- What reward are you living for—earthly or eternal?

Being a citizen of the Kingdom of God is not always easy—but it is always worth it.

It costs your comfort, your pride, your plans, your sin. But in return, it gives you peace, purpose, power, and eternal joy. It gives you the King Himself.

Let the world keep its treasures. You have a better inheritance.

So, take up your cross. Follow the King. Live with no regrets. For in the end, you will hear the words every citizen longs for:

"Well done, good and faithful servant… Come and share your Master's happiness." (Matthew 25:23)

M. C. BROWN

Chapter 13

BECOMING A CITIZEN TODAY

There comes a moment in every journey when a decision must be made—a crossroads between wandering and belonging, between exile and home. This is that moment.

All throughout this book, we've explored the contrast between being a spiritual refugee—lost, disconnected, and seeking shelter—and a Kingdom citizen—anchored in Christ, adopted by the Father, and filled with the Spirit.

But the question remains: How do you become a citizen of the Kingdom of God?

It is not a status earned by effort or inherited by birth. It is a gift of grace, received by faith, and sealed by the Spirit.

This chapter is your invitation—to lay down your refugee status and step into the glorious reality of life as a citizen of heaven.

1. Recognize Your Refugee Status

The first step is honest self-awareness. Before anyone can become a citizen of the Kingdom, they must realize they are living outside of it. *"For all have sinned and fall short of the glory of God." (Romans 3:23)*

Spiritual refugees are not just those who feel lost—they are those who are lost. We were created to live under the rule and care of God, but we wandered away, choosing independence over intimacy.

You must admit:

- I've been living by my own rules.
- I've been far from the presence of God.
- I need forgiveness, direction, and a new identity.

This is not a step of shame—it's a step of truth. And truth is what sets us free.

2. Turn and Trust the King

Becoming a citizen begins not with a passport or policy, but with a Person: Jesus Christ. *"I am the way and the truth and the life. No one comes to the Father except through me." (John 14:6)*

To enter the Kingdom, you must repent and believe:

- Repent: Turn away from your old way of life, from sin, self-reliance, and rebellion.

- Believe: Trust in Jesus alone for salvation—His death for your sin, His resurrection for your new life, His Lordship over your future.

Jesus is not just the gate into the Kingdom—He is the King. Will you bow your heart to Him today?

3. Receive the New Identity

Salvation is not just the forgiveness of sin—it is the beginning of a new identity. *"Yet to all who did receive him… he gave the right to become children of God." (John 1:12)*

When you give your life to Christ:

- You are born again (John 3:3).
- You become a new creation (2 Corinthians 5:17).
- You receive the Holy Spirit as a guarantee of your citizenship (Ephesians 1:13–14).
- You are transferred from the kingdom of darkness into the Kingdom of the Son (Colossians 1:13).

No more spiritual wandering. No more guessing where you belong. You are His. You are home.

4. Be Baptised and Join the Family

Kingdom citizenship is personal, but it is not private. Jesus calls us to go public with our decision. *"Repent and be baptized, every one of you, in the name of Jesus Christ for the forgiveness of your sins." (Acts 2:38)*

Baptism is an outward sign of an inward change. It is a declaration:

- I was lost, but now I'm found.
- I was a refugee, but now I'm a citizen.
- Jesus is Lord of my life.

From that moment forward, you are not only part of God's Kingdom—you are part of God's people, the Church. You are called to grow, serve, and walk alongside others in this new life.

5. Live as a Citizen—Starting Today

Citizenship is not a finish line—it's a beginning. Now that you belong to the King, you are called to:

- Know Him through prayer and Scripture.
- Obey Him even when it's hard.
- Serve Him with your gifts and time.
- Represent Him to others with your life and love.

Your life becomes a testimony. Every act of obedience is a signpost that says: "The Kingdom of God is real. And you can belong too."

6. An Invitation for You

If you've read this far and know you've been living as a spiritual refugee, the invitation is clear: Come home.

You don't need to clean yourself up. You don't need to understand everything. You just need to come with an open heart and say: "Jesus, I give You my life. I turn from my sin and receive Your grace. I want to follow You as my King. Make me a citizen of Your Kingdom."

If that's your prayer today welcome. Welcome to the Kingdom. Welcome to the family. You are no longer a stranger. You are home.

REFLECTION:

- Have you made the personal decision to follow Jesus?

- If not, what's holding you back?

- If you have, how are you living out your citizenship each day?

Citizenship in the Kingdom of God is the greatest privilege, the highest calling, and the most secure identity you will ever have.

You were never meant to live as a refugee—wandering, fearful, searching.

You were made to be a child of the King, a citizen of heaven, a builder of the Kingdom.

So, step forward in faith. Leave the exile behind. Embrace the life you were always meant to live.

The King is calling. Will you answer today?

*In the final chapter, I'll offer a clear and compassionate **invitation to Kingdom citizenship**—to those who have wandered, doubted, or never truly known what it means to belong.*

Chapter 14

AN INVITATION TO CITIZENSHIP

"Here I am! I stand at the door and knock. If anyone hears my voice and opens the door, I will come in and eat with that person, and they with me." —Revelation 3:20 (NIV)

Throughout this book, we've traced the journey of the believer—from spiritual displacement to divine belonging. From wandering refugee to established citizen. From estranged sinner to adopted son or daughter. And now we arrive at the heart of the matter: your response.

The Kingdom of God is not a theory to be studied; it is a reality to be entered. And citizenship is not automatic—it is received through faith, repentance, and surrender.

This final chapter is a personal and pastoral call: Will you say yes to full citizenship in the Kingdom of God?

1. The Invitation Is for All
The invitation to become a citizen is open to every person. No background, brokenness, or bondage can disqualify you. Jesus said: *"Whoever comes to me I will never drive away."* —John 6:37 (NIV)

This Kingdom is not built on status, education, race, or heritage. It is built on grace. All who confess Christ as King are welcomed in:

- The addicted
- The religious
- The wounded
- The wandering
- The weary

2. Christ Is the Door

Jesus didn't just speak about the Kingdom—He is the entrance into it. *"I am the gate; whoever enters through me will be saved."* —John 10:9 (NIV)

Citizenship is not earned by:

- Good deeds
- Church attendance
- Religious tradition

It is received by trusting in Jesus Christ alone—His death, His resurrection, His righteousness. Only through Him can you be born again and enter the Kingdom of God (John 3:3).

3. Repentance Is the Key

Jesus' first public words were: *"Repent, for the kingdom of heaven has come near."* —Matthew 4:17 (NIV)

To repent means to:
- Change your mind about sin and self
- Turn from your own rule
- Yield to Christ's Lordship

You cannot enter the Kingdom while clinging to your own crown. Citizenship requires surrender—but what you give up is nothing compared to what you gain.

4. You Receive Identity, Inheritance, and Intimacy

When you say yes to Christ, you are:

- Adopted into God's family (Romans 8:15)
- Sealed with the Holy Spirit (Ephesians 1:13)
- Given a new name and nature (2 Corinthians 5:17)
- Granted access to God's presence (Hebrews 4:16)
- Entrusted with Kingdom purpose (Ephesians 2:10)

You become more than a church member. You become a Kingdom citizen, with eternal rights and responsibilities.

5. It's Time to Come Home

Perhaps you've been in church for years but still feel like an outsider. Maybe you've wandered from the faith or settled for religion instead of relationship. Perhaps you've never known that the Kingdom was available to you.

This is your moment. The Father is watching. The Son has made the way. The Spirit is calling.

"Consequently, you are no longer foreigners and strangers, but fellow citizens with God's people and also members of his household." —Ephesians 2:19 (NIV)

Don't wait another day.

6. A Simple Prayer of Citizenship

If you're ready to surrender to Christ and receive your citizenship in the Kingdom, you may pray like this:

Father, I come to You today in the name of Jesus. I acknowledge that I have sinned and lived apart from You. I believe Jesus died for my sins and rose again. Today I repent, and I surrender to Your rule. Jesus, be my Saviour and my King. I receive Your forgiveness, Your grace, and Your Spirit. I declare that I am no longer a refugee. I am a citizen of the Kingdom of God. In Jesus' name, Amen.

7. Now Grow in Your Citizenship

Citizenship begins with salvation, but it continues through:

- Discipleship
- Community in a local church
- Regular time in the Word and prayer
- Service to others
- Sharing the Good News

You are now part of something bigger than yourself. Heaven celebrates your decision. The Church welcomes you. The Kingdom advances through you.

Conclusion

THE JOURNEY HOME

We have come to the end of this book—but perhaps, for you, it is just the beginning. Throughout these pages, we've traced the path from spiritual exile to Kingdom citizenship—from wandering without a home to finding belonging, purpose, and identity in Christ.

We've asked honest questions:

- Am I truly living under the rule of Christ?
- Do I merely believe in God, or have I surrendered to Him?

- Am I still living like a refugee, or have I embraced my citizenship in the Kingdom?

And we've encountered the answer again and again: The door to the Kingdom is wide open—but it is found only in Christ. *"Once you were not a people, but now you are the people of God."* (1 Peter 2:10)

This World Is Not Our Home. You may still live in a world marked by pain, brokenness, and rebellion—but as a Kingdom citizen, you are no longer defined by it.

You are:

- A child of God
- A servant of the King
- A bearer of light
- A voice of truth
- A vessel of grace

You carry the culture of heaven wherever you go. You no longer follow the patterns of this world—you walk to the beat of a different drum, led by the Spirit, grounded in the Word, driven by the love of the King.

Keep Walking. Your citizenship in God's Kingdom is not the end—it's the beginning of a lifelong journey of transformation.

Keep going. Keep growing. Keep trusting. Keep choosing the narrow road, even when it's lonely. Keep resisting the lies of the world and embracing the truth of the Gospel.

When you stumble, get up. When you doubt, pray. When you feel alone, remember the cloud of witnesses who've gone before you—and the Spirit who walks with you now.

The King who called you will never leave you.

One Day, the Kingdom Will Come in Full. Right now, we live in the "already but not yet." The Kingdom is here—but not fully revealed. We taste it, we live it, we announce it. But one day soon...

> *"...the kingdom of the world has become the kingdom of our Lord and of His Christ, and He shall reign forever and ever." (Revelation 11:15)*

One day, the skies will break open. The King will return. The refugee will no longer wander. The citizen will finally be home.

No more tears. No more sin. No more fear. Only the presence of God, the joy of His people, and the fullness of the Kingdom.

If you are still on the fence—still clinging to your independence, your fears, or your doubts—know this:

The King is calling you. Not to rules, but to relationship. Not to religion, but to resurrection. Not to fear, but to freedom.

Come as you are.

Surrender what you cannot keep to gain what you cannot lose.

The Kingdom is at hand. Are you ready to come home?

BENEDICTION:

"Now to Him who is able to keep you from falling, and to present you before His glorious presence without fault and with great joy—to the only God our Savior be glory, majesty, power and authority, through Jesus Christ our Lord, before all ages, now and forevermore! Amen." (Jude 1:24–25)

From Refugee to Royalty:

You are not an orphan. You are not an outcast. You are not a temporary guest. You are a citizen, a child, and an heir. *"The Spirit himself testifies with our spirit that we are God's children." —Romans 8:16 (NIV)*

Now live like it. Walk in it. Serve with it. Advance the Kingdom. The King has made His decree—and you have been accepted.

Welcome home.

M. C. BROWN

THE END

ABOUT THE BOOK

ARE YOU A REFUGEE OR A CITIZEN IN THE KINGDOM OF GOD is a profound spiritual exploration of identity, belonging, and purpose in God's Kingdom. Through the powerful metaphor of refugees and citizens, Bishop M. C. Brown challenges readers to examine where they truly stand in their relationship with God.

This book offers a deeply biblical and pastoral journey, from spiritual exile and wandering to full citizenship and authority in Christ. It unpacks the difference between merely attending church and living as a rooted, empowered citizen of Heaven. With rich scriptural insight, it exposes the refugee mindset, marked by insecurity, disconnection, and survival, and offers a path to restoration, belonging, and transformation.

Whether you feel distant from God, weary from religious performance, or hungry for deeper purpose, this book is a call to return, be restored, and live boldly under the reign of Christ. It's more than a message; it's an invitation to come home.

REFUGEE OR CITIZEN?

M. C. BROWN

www.ingramcontent.com/pod-product-compliance
Lightning Source LLC
Chambersburg PA
CBHW052037070526
44584CB00016B/2074